Lord, Is This a Psalm?

Other books

Poetry

Correspondence Between the Stonehaulers
Sonnets from the Puerto Rican

Fiction

Dominoes and Other Stories

Translation

Song of the Simple Truth: The Collected Poems of Julia de Borgos

Lord, Is This a Psalm?

Jack Agüeros

Hanging Loose Press
Brooklyn, New York

Published by Hanging Loose Press, 231 Wyckoff Street, Brooklyn, NY 11217-2208. All rights reserved. No part of this book may be reproduced without the publisher's written permission, except for brief quotations in reviews.

www.hangingloosepress.com

Printed in the United States of America
109 8 7 6 5 4 3 2 1

Hanging Loose Press thanks the Literature Program of the New York State Council on the Arts for a grant in support of the publication of this book.

Cover photograph by Frank Espada
Cover design by Ben Piekut

Acknowledgments: Some of these poems first appeared in *Boston Review, Compost, Massachusetts Review, Tercer Milenio* and *Verse*. Some also appeared in the collections *Correspondence Between the Stonehaulers* and *Sonnets from the Puerto Rican*.

Library of Congress Cataloging-in-Publication Data

Agüeros, Jack
    Lord, is this a Psalm/Jack Agüeros.
        p.cm.
    ISBN 1-931236-06-2 (cloth) -- ISBN 1-931236-05-4 (pbk)
    1. Puerto Rico--Poetry. I. Title.

PS3551.G845 L67 2002
811.54--dc21

Produced at The Print Center, Inc. 225 Varick St., New York, NY 10014, a non-profit facility for literary and arts-related publications. (212) 206-8465

Contents

Lord, Is This a Psalm?

Lord, Is This a Psalm ?

Lord,
is this a Psalm?

If I don't sing it right,
or if I'm out of tune,
do you listen?

Lord,
I don't know how to play a harp
or any other instrument.
Best I can do is whistle,
but when I whistle I can't speak or sing.

And Lord,
will you listen even if it doesn't
praise you? Can't you take
a little nose tweaking?
You must have a sense of humor;
how else can you explain
all the goofiness on earth?

So Lord,
I say these are Psalms,
I say you should hear them,
and if you don't like them
don't worry—
I'm writing others,
I'm writing more.

Psalm for Loneliness

Lord,
I'm lonely.

21 grown persons
and one child
surround me
but still I'm lonely.

Loneliness
is like a sudden wind
that fills my sails
and blows me to the edge
of the flat world
where there is nothing to do
but hang on dumbly.

But Lord,
I'm grateful,
Thank you.
At least I'm hanging on.

Psalm for Equations

I am sleeping in Detroit, Lord,
and I am afraid
of this American Town.

The Algiers Motel is here
and I am afraid the dead will ask
"What went wrong, what
human deed gave such offense, or
terrified them into a response of fire?"

Lord, you need a new
Angel of Explanations
and a new Angel of Equations
because the dead blacks
far outnumber
the credible police.

Psalm for Archangels

Lord,
consider with me for a minute
the four Archangels.

One of them wields a sword and kills snakes.
One of them blows a horn and kills people.
One of them walks around with a fish.
One of them has been banished for 400 years.
They are all men.

Lord,
this is a good time to
remove the glass cloud
and review your hiring practices.

Psalm for the Next Millennium

Lord,
I dreamt it was the year 3001
and we still didn't know
what to do with homeless people,
poor people, odd people, or sick people.

So City Hall
paid for a giant flying saucer and filled it with
the Strange, the Homeless, the Left-Handed,
the Ill, the Poor, the Poor, the Poor,
and the people who combed their hair this way
instead of that way, and a few more poor.

And I was ordered to fly them out and
leave them anywhere but here.

And I did, because in the year 3001
we all wore T-shirts that said
"ME! ME! ME!"
and on the back "GREED IS GOOD."

But every time I got near a new planet
angry aliens screamed, "not in our galaxy," "not in our
solar system"
"not in our Milky Way," "not on our Super Nova,"
so I sped back to earth, and mistakenly landed in City
        Hall Park
where all the policemen were racial profiling for
        minority astronauts
and they nailed me for double parking,
jaywalking and Speaking Spanish
because in my excitement I said, *Caramba Karajo!*

Lord, don't laugh,
double parking carried the death penalty,
jaywalking called for the confiscation
of both my feet and all my toes,

Speaking Spanish was punishable by the
murderous sentence of English Only,
and when I went before the judge
he looked like my current mayor
and he was washing his hands
and I repeated, *"Caramba, Karajo,"* and woke up.

But Lord,
I woke up sad instead of happy,
and I woke up wondering
if it might not be better
wandering in outer space
than living in this world
where I'm supposed to ignore
the everywhere — I — look facts:
a few rich have most of the wealth
and the poor have all the poverty.

Psalm for the Onion

Lord,
thank you for the onion.
It isn't made of anything
except itself, over and over.

The onion is so much itself
that everyone wants it at
their parties.

Carrots, cabbage, peppers,
omelets, stews, soups,
everybody says, "Hello onion
so happy you could come,
glad to see ya."

And Lord,
the onion is so good
that when I work with it,
I cry.

Psalm for Open Clouds and Windows

Lord,
reserve a place for me in heaven on a cloud
with Indians, Blacks, Jews, Irish, Italians,
Portuguese and lots of Asians and Arabs, and Hispanics.

Lord,
I don't mind if they play
their music too loudly,
or if they leave their windows open—
I like the smell of ethnic foods.

But Lord,
if heaven isn't integrated,
and if any Angels are racists,
I swear I'm going to be a no-show
because, Lord,
I have already seen hell.

Psalm: A Man Grows Old

Lord,
A father gets old
when he takes his two daughters
for Sunday brunch.

At the diner,
the smaller child envisions a cave
under the table and between
the banquettes and so under she goes
because she is a bear.

Her sister, older, knows the game,
and visits the zoo, feeding the bear
under the table, bread with butter.

The father gets old,
sits there slightly shocked,
and from my booth I see the gray
hair rising on his scalp,
deep furrows forming
on his brow.

So I lean over and, butting in, say,
"Sir, you will miss this sooner than you think."

But Lord,
from his look, I see that he is not ready
for my wisdom.

Say Lord,
Isn't that
sort of how it is between Thee and me?

Psalm: Another Man Grows Old

Lord,
I know what makes a man grow old:
it's the looking back and forth
between his paycheck
and his checkbook,
his checkbook
and his paycheck.

Psalm for Peace

Lord,
why isn't there an Angel of Peace?

The Angel of War
eats money and blood,
is too successful
has too many passports,
too many followers,
too many holes in the ground.

Where is that Dove of yours?

Lord,
all I see is vultures.

Psalm for Emily Dickinson

Lord,
Emily Dickinson spoke so nicely to me
that I went to visit her grave.

On her stone was incised:

"Emily Dickinson,
Called Back."

Lord,
I wanted to add,
"You also stayed with us."
But Lord,
how could I revise her writing?

Psalm: Why I'm Annoyed

Lord,
sometimes after readings
people ask me why
I'm so annoyed with you.

Lord,
I always answer truthfully:
it's because you don't take or answer my calls.

Psalm: My Resignation

Lord,
my parents drafted me into a faith
they never practiced.

Before I was even fourteen
men in long black skirts
and women in starched faces
said I was certified.

But Lord, they spoke too soon,
the Holy Water dried behind my ears
and I am thinking of resigning
because I can't belong to anything
that keeps women down and out.

Psalm for Modernization

Lord,
the New Jersey Bishops
went to see the Governor.

They are not opposed
to state-sponsored gambling—
they just don't like
that it cuts into their
Bingo take.

Lord,
I say we gotta modernize,
sing hymns and chant the daily numbers,
and what about a slot machine
that will pay big
if you hit three bleeding hearts of Jesus?

Psalm: Those Flags

Lord,
I am the animal that erects tall poles
and stakes them in the ground.

Lord,
I am the animal that makes flags
and flies and flaunts them.
Puts poles on the sides of streets and
on top of tall buildings. Raises telegraphs
and antennas, microwaves, radio and television,
launches satellites on long, tall rockets,
and puts flags on moons and planets,
and makes everything ever taller and taller
and way, way up, on top,
those flags,
those troublesome troublesome problematical
flying flopping flags,
those ideological flags,
those flags, flags, flags,
those freaking, freaking, flags.

Psalm for the Damnation of Pig Pino Oink Ochet, Who Unlike His Victims Will Neither Die nor Disappear, Because He Was Never Human.

Pig Pino oink ochet,
your body's not dead yet
your body will not die
and we will never bury you or your name
for it will become a synonym
for puke, for murderer, for vileness,
for desecration, for depravity.

Pig Pino oink ochet,
your body will not decompose
because the sensible bacteria shudder
and will not touch your hideous corpse,
and the worms will run from your grave
as if death squads pursued them,
and the worms will starve rather than take
a taste of your wretched remains.

Around your grave,
Pig Pino oink ochet,
no grass will grow, because your body
will not become fertilizer,
and forever the ground will be sterile
from the poison you planted in Chile.

Pig Pino oink ochet,
your name will enter the dictionary
in the definition of villainy, of moral rot,
of everything putrid and nauseating.

And rather than face
the possibility of having to forgive you
no one will ever
want to be God.

Psalm for My *Pilón*

Lord,
you placed a wooden
chalice in my kitchen,
my mortar, my *pilón*.

I mashed millions
of garlic cloves,
poured oceans of olive oil,
sprinkled whole forests of
oregano leaves
and now they all live in the wood
like sap in a tree
blood in my veins.
Sometimes when I am hungry
I stick my nose in that *pilón*
and inhale and raise it over my head.

Lord, then Angels rush to my side,
ring bells and set tables,
open the dam on my salivary glands,
and together our spirits dine
on aroma alone.

Psalm for Movies and Television

Lord,
in the movies
you can kill as many people as you like,
by any means you like
fast or slow, if you like,
shooting, stabbing, choking, drowning, blowing up,
if you like,
especially shooting, shooting, shooting, shooting, shooting,
shooting, shooting, shooting,
which we like.

But Lord,
don't worry,
we don't let the kids see these movies.
They watch television.

Psalm for the Motion Picture Classification and Rating Administration

(This Psalm Is Rated "Parental Discretion")

Lord, here are the rules for the movies:
Man on top of woman is okay.
Woman on top of man is not okay!
Woman on top or bottom of woman is not okay!
Frontal erect penises are not okay!
Moving butts in sex is not okay!
Moving butts on girls in very tiny tiny tiny tiny
bikinis shot in close-up from behind, is okay!
Fuck used as adverb or adjective is not okay.
Examples:
Saying "Fuck you," is not okay.
Saying "Fuck off," is okay.

Lord,
thank goodness
these rules are only for the movies.
In life
everything is okay.

28

Psalm: Rent A Nun

Lord,
I can rent a nun.

For one hundred American bucks
I can get a nun
who will pray for me all year long.

Lord, with a nun on my side
I can get those things I wanted—
that special dame I been waiting for,
a cat that won't scratch me and make me sneeze,
a raise, a winning ticket at the lottery.

But Lord,
in case it doesn't work,
and my prayers don't get answered,
who is the Angel in charge of Consumer Fraud?

Source: Article with dateline of Los Angeles, 16 Feb 1997, reported in
El Diario/La Prensa, p. 13: *Silesian Sisters of San Juan Bosco have raised
$275,000 charging $100 a year to pray for the buyer, with a goal of $5
million to build a home for the nuns.*

Psalm for Unanswered Questions

Lord,
do cockroaches like pickles?
Do mice enjoy tuna fish?
Do rats say "hi" to each other
when they meet on subway platforms?

Do flies consider swatters
cruel and unusual punishment?
Are mosquitoes ever vegetarians?
Do silkworms ever rebel
and make Lycra?
Do bees go on strike,
demand salt in the commissary?
Do centipedes ever break legs,
use crutches, wear braces,
ride wheelchairs?

Lord, when I die
will the library in heaven
have answers to these questions?

Will there be a library?
Lord, there's gotta be a library!

Psalm: Who's Mugging Who?

Lord, the children mug us
for video games
portable radios
leather jackets
gravity-defying sneakers
large gold earrings
automobiles
super boom boxes
designer chemicals
and other Admirable American Advertising
Gotta-Haves.

Lord,
arrest the Angel of Economics,
and put the Angel of Advertising
in rehab:
I accuse them of mugging the kids.

Psalm for Popularizing Death

Lord, your busy porter Death
is very misunderstood.

Death needs a public relations firm
to work up an appropriate image.

Let's get rid of that dark ding-dong stuff,
put an Armani over those bones,
and a rakish scarf,
cast away that scythe
give him a nice shiny black pistol
and black leather gloves
like all the adults have in the movies
and all the children on my block.

And Lord, what about
an Angelic Chorus
with an eclectic repertoire
of Doo-Wop, Gospel, and Rap
to accompany Death—
while he brings us
your big favor?

Psalm for Scrutability

Lord,
for too many years
you've sat hidden in your holy chair
behind your opaque celestial door.

Noting your golden silence
an industry of black- and red-robed
translators and interpreters
boldly allege they speak for you.

Lord,
the time has come
for plain talk and declarative sentences.
Put aside the ambiguous parables,
and please,
be scrutable!

Psalm for Infectious Love

Lord,
I cling to her lost love
as if it was a big log
and I try to carve it into a canoe.

Lord,
I know you make infectious love—
where do you keep the antidote?

Psalm for the Christian Who Didn't Want the Gay and Lesbian Parade to March in Front of St. Patrick's Cathedral, NYC, 19 June, 1995

Lord,
I know that the altar
is a sacred part of a cathedral,
and since they all touch each other,
I guess the aisle and the pews
and the doors and the front steps
and the sidewalk in front
are sacred too.

Lord,
I never thought about it before
but the curbstone is sacred
and the gutter is sacred
and the roadbed is sacred
and the atoms that make up the tar
are sacred.

So, Lord,
explain to me,
how can any of earth's children
not be sacred?

Psalm for Women

Lord,
thank you for making women.
Thank you for giving me eyes
to see them, nose to smell them,
fingers to turn their pages slowly,
tongue to taste them,
sweet moments to entangle our curly hair.

Thank you for making them
the superior gender,
for filling them with understanding
that I never understood.

And Lord, listen,
I personally don't believe in sin,
but please forgive me
if I ever wronged a woman.

Psalm: Lord You Giveth But ...

Lord, I am sad tonight
because tomorrow
I will wake up in a state
that has the Death Penalty again.

Lord,
remember the saying—
the Lord giveth and the Lord taketh away?

It's been rewritten—
now the Lord giveth,

The Governor and the Mayor
taketh away.

Psalm for Bottles and Cans

Lord,
street people are brittle as bottles
and collapsible as cans.

But Lord,
think about it,
bottles and cans are redeemable
bottles and cans are refillable
bottles and cans have cash value
but street people have
only our contempt.

Psalm for Distribution

Lord,
on 8th Street
between 6th Avenue and Broadway
in Greenwich Village
there are enough shoe stores
with enough shoes
to make me wonder
why there are shoeless people
on the earth.

Lord,
You have to fire the Angel
in charge of distribution.

Psalm for *Pasteles*

Lord,
everybody thinks that after you made the world
you took a day off.
But I think that on the seventh day
you created *pasteles*.

I know it took you all day,
dicing pork and beef,
cooking olives and capers
making dough by shredding green plantains
and mashing *yucca*,
stuffing the dough
then wrapping it in plantain leaves
tying them into bow tie shapes
and boiling them for two hours
until all of heaven smelled like
my mother's kitchen at Christmas.

Lord, yes,
even you needed a whole day to make *pasteles*,
that's why they think you took a day off,
but you were steaming in the kitchen training Angels
so they could visit us with your recipes.

Lord,
thank you for the glory of *pasteles*.

40

Psalm for Your Image

Lord,
You gave the indian tobacco
You gave the white man alcohol
You gave the arab coffee
You gave the chinese gunpowder.

Lord, I can't shake the tobacco
can't leave the alcohol
can't imagine a world
without coffee.

And as for the gunpowder,
which I could do without,
it's always popping around me.

Lord,
if we are in your image
you must be a coffee-guzzling
gunslinger with a serious hangover
and a cigarette cough.

Psalm: Spanish Forever!

Lord,
some people
do not like my tongue.
They find it too flexible,
accuse me of having an accent,
say my tongue is a racehorse
and that it laughs too loudly.

They want to pass a language law
put my tongue in jail with my culture
who is my loyal accomplice.
The next time they hear me say
Ay bendito, cuchifrito, Puerto Rico
they will charge me with seditious conspiracy
and sentence me to English Only.

But don't worry, Lord,
when they ask me how I plead
I will raise my fist and shout
Spanish Forever!,
and as they drag me down
the imperial corridors
I will be heard singing
my bilingual national anthem—
Ay bendito, cuchifrito, Puerto Rico
Spanish Forever!

Psalm: For Patience

Lord,
Hurry up and give me patience!

Psalm for Equal Opportunity

Lord,
Is heaven another stratified society?

You, like a king or dictator on top,
a lower phalanx of cherubim,
then the three Archangels
plus the one or two that seem to be
persona non grata,
then Saints,
then holy people,
then plain old nice folks?

Do the plain folks ever get to see you?
Do they have to call bureaucratic
secretaries, Saints and Archangels
to get appointments with you?
Do you deliver a public speech on
the state of the Heavens each year?

Can anybody live on your cloud?

Lord,
is there equal opportunity
to glorify you?

Psalm for My Death

Lord,
when I die, let Death meet me
in November at 4 pm
with the sun in Manhattan
warming the red brick buildings.

Let Death be a night in October
with the full harvest moon.

Let it be April, Spring sticking its gorgeous toes
in the water of New York Harbor,
let me be the Ferry Boat Ghost
patrolling the outer deck.

Lord, send me any of these deaths:
That will be heaven enough for me.

Psalm: Did You Make Hell?

Lord,
if you made the universe
then you are good.

If you made Hell,
then you're just like the rest of us.

Psalm: Mugger Moods

Lord,
sometimes a mood
grabs me by the neck
and like a mugger in the night
throws me to the ground.

Suddenly I'm down
missing her again
and angry with myself
for missing her.

Lord,
is there an
Angel for the lonely?

Psalm: the New Jersey Bishops Again

Lord, the New Jersey Bishops
are outraged again.

Yes, they went complaining to the Governor
that no-smoking laws
make it hard to fill Bingo halls.

Lord, can't you send Jesus
to turn over a few tables
in the temples?

Psalm for the Pope's Limousines

Lord,
I read that the Pope has a Mercedes Benz,
and I read that the Pope
has another Mercedes Benz
and another
and another
and Lord, I read
that the Pope has
still one more—
a fifth
Mercedes Benz.

Source: *New York Times*, 7 Mar 1997, p. B2, Metro Section

Psalm for Equations

I am sleeping in Detroit, Lord,
and I am afraid
of this American Town.

The Algiers Motel is here
and I am afraid the dead will ask
"What went wrong, what
human deed gave such offense, or
terrified them into a response of fire?"

Lord, you need a new
Angel of Explanations
and a new Angel of Equations
because the dead blacks
far outnumber
the credible police.

Psalm for the World Restaurant

Lord, the Angel in charge
of the World Restaurant
has a weird menu ...

one page has no food,
one page has half portions,
one page is all chemical killers.

Lord, I know these are serious charges,
but stuffing his face with raw profits
has destroyed his taste buds.

Lord, cancel his subscription
to *Gourmet Magazine*.

Psalm for *Tostones*

Lord,
I love *tostones.*
Where else could they come from
but your celestial kitchen?

I can see you now, Lord,
finest slicer in the universe,
cutting half-inch rings of green plantains.

I can see your blazing luminosity
heating oil in the celestial frying pan.

I can see the *sous chef* Angel
flattening *tostones* with his heavenly hands
and refrying them and making them gloriously golden.

Lord,
my mouth waters when I smell *tostones,*
my eyes water when I see *tostones,*
my mouth hums hymns when I eat *tostones,*
and Lord, no lie,
when I eat *tostones,* I feel Holy!

Psalm for Rice and Beans

Lord,
thank you for rice
and for marrying it to beans.
Especially for rice
which doesn't grow much in Puerto Rico,
especially for yellow rice,
colored and flavored with saffron
and when saffron got more expensive
than cocaine,
thank you for *achiote*
also known as *annatto*,
the poor man's saffron
which still makes the rice yellow and tasty.
And thank you for kidney beans—
they don't grow much in Puerto Rico either
but we sure know how to cook them there.

Lord,
thank you for making me rich
in rice and beans
and for the luxurious wealth
of avocados.

Lord,
I know you are expecting
one of my smart-ass closings,
but Lord, I mean this,
thank you for low fat,
no cholesterol, low priced,
easy to prepare,
super tasty,
rice and beans!

Psalm for Nutrition

Lord,
The Angel in charge of Nutrition
is energetic and smart,
but he's seriously mixed up.

He thinks he's supposed to hawk
hunger, additives, and junk food,
so he's helping to create franchises
where people pay
to gain weight and lose health.

Lord,
send the Angel of Nutrition
into the desert, and put him
on 40 days of bread and water.

Meanwhile, how about cloud-arrest
For the Angel of Franchises?

Psalm: Homosexual Catch-22

Lord,
The International
Theological Commission
has ruled that if homosexuals are chaste
they may participate in the path of
sanctification like all Christians.

Lord,
seems to me that
over at the Vatican
the prolonged exposure
to incense and candle smoke
is causing hallucinatory declarations.

Source, *L'Osservatore Romano*, as quoted in *El Diario/La Prensa*, p. 15,
27 Apr 1997.

Psalm for My Favorite American Speech

Lord,
I have read many American Speeches,
and I have heard far too many American Speeches,

Still, I do have an all time favorite American Speech.
It's this one:

"No, I will not go to the back of the bus."

Thank you, Ms. Rosa Parks.

Psalm: The Heaven I Want

Lord,
when I die I want Heaven to be
New York City
with many people
speaking many languages fast
and ethnic cooking in hundreds of restaurants
and many mixed marriages and noisy ethnic children

and Lord,
if you can do it,
Heaven should have
subways that run
almost on time.

Psalm for Uriel

Lord,
whatever became of the
Archangel Uriel?

He used to be in charge
of interpreting judgments and prophecies—
did he screw up big,
did you quietly demote and banish him?

We haven't seen a picture of him
since the Renaissance, and he gets no press:
Is he in eternal rehabilitation
or did you terminate him with prejudice?

Psalm: Why Death Is Long

Lord,
I understand this now:
Life is such a feast
so full of super-dishes
sweet and hot surprises,
salads and sumptuous desserts,
steamy and salty stews spicy as sex,
occasional soups that go sour,
and such an abundance of tastes
and tales, travail and blunders
and laughter,
that we need a long quiet
Death to digest it all.

Psalm for My Faith

Lord, it's not true
that my faith is cooling.
It's just that people
are saying that candle smoke
has caused cancer in church mice.
and I also worry that candlelight
is too weak to reach your cloud.

Do I need a hydrogen candle?
Are the Angels into lasers?

Lord, as I think about it,
lately I haven't had much to thank you for.

Are you on vacation?

Psalm for Depression

Lord,
the Angel of Depression
is very effective.
When the great shadow of his wings
falls over me,
it squeezes and smothers and turns off the lights
and like an octopus
it tangles me in its tentacles
and paralyzes me.

Lord,
I want to send hosannas
to the Angel who frees me—

who is it?

Psalm for the Pope's Five License Plates

Lord,
I have suggestions for the Pope's
Five license plates
for his Five Mercedes Limousines.

Big Guy.
Holy 1.
El Papa.
Pure-issimo.

Lord,
I know that's only four,
but I'm withdrawing
Humble 1,

because it doesn't seem to fit.

Psalm: Proof of Your Divinity

Lord,
a woman's breast
is one of your great inspirations,
and the fact that you gave
each woman two breasts
is proof you are Divine.

Psalm: A Woman Grows Old

Lord,
A woman gets old
taking the weight of a grapefruit
in her hand. I see her in the market
seesawing her hand up and down,
bending her elbow, cradling the globe.

In the swing of that arc,
she feels for the right one,
the juicy one, the ripe one, the sweet-smelling one,
the one that talks to her instinct.

Weighing fruit and vegetables alone could take
one-seventh of her life, cooking and diapers
easily take another seventh of her life,
but these are not chores, nor burden, nor sacrifice.

Because Lord,
appraising fruit and vegetables
is one of the happy exercises of love for her family,
and while it's true that she grows older
she also becomes ageless
exercising love.

Psalm for Redesign

Lord, could you talk
to the Angel in Charge of Design?

If we were meant to be shot up in wars,
saloons, and subways, we need exo-skeletons
like lobsters have,
but in bulletproof chain mail.

We are the only animal who sleeps on cement,
doorways, sidewalks and stairwells.
Why didn't we each get our own house
like snails have on their backs?

Lord, could you also wake up the
Angel of Compassion?

Psalm for Gratification

Lord,
I'm told that the trouble
with us minorities
is that we seek instant gratification.

But Lord,
it ain't us promoting
cell phones, fast food,
instant cash and credit,
and Concorde jets to fetch them!

Psalm for *Bochinche*

Lord,
When the New York Times does it,
it's called "news."
When the National Enquirer does it
it's called "Tabloid Trash."
When Daniel Shorr does it,
it's called "analysis," or "punditry."
When Geraldo does it
it's called "investigative reporting."
When a professor does it,
it's called "commentary."
When a sportscaster does it
it's called "background."
When radio does it
it's called a "breaking story."
When television does it
it's called "Hard Copy."

And Lord, when my neighbor,
Juana Fulana de la Palangana does it,
we all call it *"Bochinche."*

Psalm for *Bacalao*

Lord,
thank you for *bacalao,*
thank you for salted *bacalao*
and thank you for boneless *bacalao*
and thank you for *bacalao*
which is so amenable that
it swims in tomato sauce as happily
as it swims in olive oil.

Lord,
thank you especially for *bacalao*
since it doesn't swim anywhere
near Puerto Rico.
Thank you for making it go good
with green bananas
onion rings and scrambled eggs.

And Lord,
since it's a fish
thank you for letting it fly
to Puerto Rico, thank you
for letting it ride on boats
into our harbors, thank you
for letting it swim in our happy mouths.

Psalm for *Coquito*

Lord, it was Christmas time,
and I was drinking homemade
Coquito,
a nog with coconut milk and rum,
condensed and evaporated milk and rum,
cloves, eggs, more rum, nutmeg, cinnamon
and a little more rum,
and I was reading the daily newspapers.

I read Exxon and Mobil had merged
proudly firing thousands of people
and expunging the word "oligarchy"
from the dictionary.
I thought Olivetti made typewriters
but I read it was really in optical fibers,
and a German bank was buying an
American bank, even though the
American bank was being sued
for stealing money from Jews
during the Holocaust.
The old Philadelphia Car Battery Company
and Campbell's Soup and Heinz Ketchup
had reorganized and were now making
hostile intercontinental ballistic missiles.

Lord, my mistake was not in drinking the rum,
my mistake was reading the newspapers,
because that night, Lord, I had a dream
that our national motto was now
"Where's Mine?"
and that a dark-skinned family was evicted
from a manger in the South Bronx
and the brilliantly named
Department of Wealth Acquisition
sent them to the only Municipal Shelter
where there were no beds or blankets

but José got Prozac,
María got Methadone,
and Baby Jesus got scolded for not having a job yet.

Psalm for Amadou Diallo*

Amadou Diallo
1, 2, 3, 4, 5, 6, 7 ??

Amadou Diallo
8, 9, 10, 11, 12, 13, 14,

Amadou Diallo
15, 16, 17, 18, 19, 20, 21,

Amadou Diallo
22, 23, 24, 25, 26, 27, 28,

Amadou Diallo
29, 30, 31, 32, 33, 34, 35,

Amadou Diallo
36, 37, 38, 39, 40, 41,

Amadou Diallo
41,?

Amadou Diallo
41, 41, 41!

*Unarmed, shot by 4 cops firing 41 bullets, killed. Feb, 1999, in the South Bronx, Sound View area. All cops found innocent of murder or manslaughter, the Year of our Lord 2000.

Psalm: Fierce Mike, Archangel

Lord,
You have delegated judgments
to the fierce Archangel Michael
who wears a bulletproof vest
menaces with a sword and spears
dubiously calibrates his scales
and has a thing against serpents.

And Lord, I'm a pacifist,
and, since you made them,
I think snakes are cool.

Lord, I don't want to be judged
by Fierce Mike,
I think he lays a fat thumb on those scales,
and Fierce Mike wouldn't hesitate
to throw me in the snake pit.

Lord,
you see, I'm familiar with hanging judges
like Fierce Mike—
He won't read me my rights,
so Lord, please tell me
who is the Angel of Appeals?

Psalm Welcoming Death

Lord,
when my time comes
send Kissing Death,
whose lips are cool and kind like the morning wind;

send Musical Death,
who gets bass fiddle notes twanging the life chord;
send Running Death
who barefoot breaks the one-minute mile;

send Chopper Death of the single blow;
or Surgeon Death of the silent slice.

Lord, please don't send that
off-and-on-again-
can't-make-up-his-mind-when Death

because Lord,
I'm eager to see you,
eager to tell you how
things ought to be.